Lashonna!

Phenomenal
WOMAN...
Gurl That's U!

Thanks so much for all your support! Your letter is in the teen version coming next month! I appreciate you

----

BY DAGNE BARTON

----

so much! Love you!

Dagne Barton

Phenomenal WOMAN… Gurl That's U!

Dagne Barton

Phenomenal Woman…Gurl That's U!

TABLE OF CONTENTS

DEDICATION

This is the first book I authored. It is dedicated to the author and finisher of my faith – Jesus Christ.

It is also dedicated in loving memory of the original MuhDear – Janie Thompkins and "GrandDaddy" and "Momma Johnnie" John, Sr. & Johnnie B. Kendrick.

Finally, it is dedicated to every person that has ever encouraged me. There are too many to name that have done that over my lifetime, and especially leading up to this endeavor.

If you are one of those, whom I hold dear, you know who you are because you're smiling right now.

You know who you are because you're feeling proud right at this very moment as you read this.

This is dedicated to you.

ACKNOWLEDGEMENTS

I want to thank my husband, the love of my life, Isadore Barton, Jr., who from the first moment I met him has been my greatest encourager. Babe you have made me feel the most loved, the most protected, the most desired, the most covered I have ever felt. You are the greatest part of my day and I am honored to be your wife.

I want to thank my children — Charles — my A1 since day 1 — we have been in this thing together and I love you so much — thanks for always being there for me. Carmen — my girl! I didn't give birth to you, but from the day I said I do to your "my daddy" I loved you and considered you my first daughter. I am so proud of you and you inspire me to do this and more! Thanks for always pushing me to go for it. Thank you and love you Ronny and Teil for accepting me into your lives with open arms. I love you Cameron, Cayelon, Cayla, Jace, Rae, and Brice… thanks for loving me and making me a GrandDaggy!

I want to thank my family — my mom Caroline, my dad Donald, my Auntie Pat, my Uncle Ronnie, Uncle John, Uncle Clarence, Uncle James, Uncle Michael, Uncle Nate and Uncle Kevin, my siblings Squirrel, Kendra & Lacresha and all of my first cousins (my first friends). Know that I love you all and I am so proud to be connected to this legacy of love!

Finally I want to thank all of the LifeChangers but in particular:
My fellow New Life Staff (paid & unpaid) — I love you guys and thank God we get to change lives together every day! My BFF Vivian for being the best cheerleader and confidant a girl could have! My Admin Anne who ADDs value to me every day! My First Lady Glenda for imparting wisdom and speaking into my life with love. AND MY Bishop, my spiritual father, my boss, my confidant, my encourager and more. Thanks for always speaking life into me, believing in me and allowing me to be a part of your SHINE day after day!

INTRODUCTION

When my son was younger, he was invited to participate in a Jr. Phenom Basketball Camp in Arizona. I was so excited because this was a great opportunity to learn from some of the best basketball minds in the country. Typically a "Phenom Camp" is the development skills camp you absolutely want your athletic children to get invited to. There are usually former professional basketball players and coaches available for a week of working on making the "already great athlete" an even better athlete. They take the natural skills and make them instinctively sharper. They help these "Junior Phenoms" break bad habits. They help them develop muscle memory with new techniques to improve their level of play. It is a great investment.

In this book, I use the backdrop of the poem by Maya Angelou, "Phenomenal Woman" to explore topics that every woman can see themselves either struggling or thriving with. I, along with some other sisters, will attempt to encourage you with each line. I will attempt to do what the Phenom camps do and take an "already great woman" and make her feel greater. I will attempt to encourage that part of you that is not so sure about your natural tendencies and help you see you're on the right path. I will use my own pitfalls and detours to help you break some poor habits. I will challenge you in some areas of weakness. I will help you form some "Mind Muscle" memory around the truth that you are a woman – phenomenally – Phenomenal Woman – GURL That's U! I believe everything we need is available in a little encouragement. I want reading this to boost your self-esteem. The knowledge of who you are in Christ and the ability to walk in all that entails is my goal for every one of us.

To break up the poem we are going look at the poem in its four stanzas – or four quarters. In Phenom Camps, they train the players how to perform in any given game in various areas of strength. Sometimes it's shooting, or dribbling, or guarding, or rebounding, or even simply passing the ball. Each of the four stanzas hit various areas of strength we possess as women. Some of them teach us something about ourselves we want to improve; some of them highlight an area where we can celebrate success. As you read the book, I suggest you break it up in order to have time to fully receive the encouragement you deserve; time to embrace the empowerment you need and time to reflect on your own places of phenomenal. There are several places for you to make notes for your Phenomenal Self!

As women, I believe the sooner we understand the inside…the wonderfully and fearfully…the better. Anything great about you, anything great about me, was pre-planned by God. Before anyone knew who Dagne was; before anyone knew who you were - God had already laid out a plan and purpose for your life. He put the wonderfully and fearfully on the inside from day one. The moment that his impartation of the shine and your acceptance and embrace of the shine met is the moment when "phenomenal" took place. My goal in this book is to help you get to your phenomenal, but it starts with embracing your shine. No two are alike. Your SHINE is the

- **S**PECIAL
- **H**APPENING
- **I**NSIDE
- **N**OBODY
- **E**LSE!

The moment we embrace IT, accept IT, and stop coveting the IT in some other woman, that's the day phenomenal takes place. Once that happens; once you get it; pay it forward and honor it in another sister! Speaking of other sisters….

I asked several other Phenomenal Women to give me their take on this great poem to encourage others. Many of them told me reflecting on a line or two in the poem was therapeutic for them. I thank God for them since it's no way I could effectively encourage ALL women with this concept without reaching beyond my own narrow thoughts. Thank you to my sisters (check out their BIOs in the appendix) for reaching inside your SHINE, connecting with my SHINE, and together illuminating some much needed light in some areas of darkness. I and these powerful ladies are coming from our own stories and experiences as examples as they reveal themselves through the words of the poem. The let the truth of our lives and the truth of God's word reveal some things to you as you take this journey! It is my prayer you find many truths to combat any lie that may be tearing you down right now! Find your shine while reading this book! Don't linger in those areas of discouragement. You have too much Special Happening Inside Nobody Else! Phenomenal Woman, Gurl That's U!

Notes to My Phenomenal Self:

FIRST QUARTER

Pretty women wonder where my secret lies.
I'm not cute or built to suit a fashion model's size
But when I start to tell them
They think I'm telling lies.
I say, It's in the reach of my arms,
The span of my hips,
The stride of my step,
The curl of my lips.
I'm a woman Phenomenally.
Phenomenal woman,
That's me.

THE "IT" FACTOR – IS THE SECRET

"Pretty women wonder where my secret lies." In my gathering of notes and doodling of ideas, I didn't want to start the book talking about looks. However, then it hit me about my IT Factor and your IT Factor. It occurred to me that for me, this first line is not about physical appearance. In life, it's rarely about the outward appearance. It has to do with our inside. On the days I try little harder with my Mary Kay application of my makeup; or my selection of garb for the day; or when my curls are popping just right on my head, that's just window dressing of what's happening on the inside. Regardless of how well I dress up the outside, it's the inside that's going to either shine or diminish everything that day. I didn't always understand it, but I get it now.

I'm reminded of a story about a time when my shine or my light attracted my first hater - or as we called them back in the day, a bully. In the third grade, for a period of about two months, I had a bully. She shall remain nameless because why would I give her credit at this point. Every day for almost 2 months she terrorized me. I would have to bring her my milk money. She would threaten to beat me up, and just be generally mean whenever she could. It really bothered me. It really perplexed me. All I had were friends and people who loved me. Why this girl hated me was a mystery. One day my teacher, Mrs. Cecelia Irvin, asked me to pass out some papers, as she often did. I jumped up to comply with her request as one of her favorites and I noticed that my bully - let's just call her Bailey for the purposes of my story - was looking at me sideways as usual. In that moment I got an idea. I asked Mrs Irvin if Bailey could help me. She agreed and Bailey jumped up beaming with joy to help pass out the papers. At the end of our task, I said "Wow! Bailey was a lot faster than me, wasn't she Mrs. Irvin?"

Mrs. Irvin agreed and said, "Great job Bailey." And we sat down. Bailey turned around and smiled at me for the first time in two months. You see, my shine in that classroom was getting to Bailey. I was the little administrator always helping my beloved teacher Mrs Irvin and clearly that was getting on Bailey's nerves. The only way she knew how to deal with her lack of shine was to terrorize me. Bailey and I never became good friends or anything, but that was the last day she took my milk money. That day when I shared my shine with her – by bringing her into the light, Mrs. Irvin started calling on her to help out sometimes as well. Just like that, it was over. My Uncle Ronnie who had been wondering why I needed extra milk money was pleased when I told him I was good to go the next day. As a third grader, I didn't know anything about my shine but Bailey did; it's what she coveted. Mrs Irvin did; it's what she bragged about to other students. But I really didn't.

That light, that shine, that "IT" factor - follows you all the days of your life. There have been "Bailey's" all your life that have seen IT in you before you did and just hated on you for no apparent reason. IT will draw people to you the rest of your life. That "IT" factor that you don't understand when it happens especially on the days when you weren't even trying. Someone may say it's just "something about you." Some days, even you don't know "where your secret lies." It's those days when you were caught showing your shine. People may simply comment on some physical aspect about you because that's what drew them to you, but in all actuality that person noticed something that was intangible about you. That person noticed something that was unreachable. That person was drawn to your SHINE. There is something to be said about a woman who understands her worth and her purpose. Do you understand yours? Use this time to reflect on that and let's do some digging for that hidden treasure.

On our dig, some of that treasure will be found in the word of God. Let's start there.

PWT: Phenomenal Woman Truth

Below are some scriptures that highlight who we are – the IT in Christ!

✓ *1 Thessalonians 1:4 - We know, brothers and sisters loved by God, that he has chosen you.*

✓ *2 Cor. 5:17 - So then, if anyone is in Christ, he is a new creation; what is old has passed away--look, what is new has come!*

✓ *John 15:15 - I no longer call you slaves, because the slave does not understand what his master is doing. But I have called you friends, because I have revealed to you everything I heard from my Father*

✓ *James 1:5 If any of you lacks wisdom, let him ask God, who gives generously to all without reproach, and it will be given him.*

Notes to My Phenomenal Self:

PWT – Phenomenal Woman Testimony

"Pretty women wonder where my secret lies"
"Pretty women wonder where my secret lies" resonated with me because when I was a kid, I always felt like I didn't belong. My sister and brother where light skinned and out spoken. We grew up in a two parent household, but our dad was gone a lot due to his job in the Army. However, when my dad was present his drill sergeant mentality continued at home. So, that in your face name calling (i.e., Fat, lazy) spilled over to my home life. Another prominent factor happened at the age of 13 when I was visiting my cousin. She said the strangest thing, "I saw your father." Looking perplexed, I said, "Nah, really me too." She said, "I'm talking about your real father." I said, "What?" Of course, I was disoriented, distorted, and felt like my life had been a lie. I confronted my parents and it was true. Now, it made sense why I was treated differently by my dad's family; why I was shorter than everyone in my immediate family; why my last name was different, and more. Now even though I found out "where my secret lies", I fell into a depression. So another part of this poem lifts me up. Phenomenal women that's me. I am telling my 13 year old self - always pray and turn your negative thoughts into positive thinking. Additionally, the only parents that you have known may have done or said some hurtful things, but forgive your parents sooner because they love you and always boast and brag about their 1st born daughter. I'm glad that today I know this to be the truth. Phenomenal Woman…That's me. **Phenom Natasha Edwards**

PWT – Phenomenal Woman Testimony

"I'm not cute or built to suit a fashion model's size" This line stood out to me. Why you ask? All my life I have found something about my body that wasn't as attractive as I believed that it should be. I was constantly measuring how I looked to the standard of the world. It is only recently that I have an understanding that health is what my focus should have always been and not on what someone else may or may not see. When you examine the outward appearance more closely, there are going to be flaws in everyone – no matter how perfect they seem. The inside of the person is what truly defines their beauty and not what appears outwardly. **Phenom Dianne Shelton**

Notes to My Phenomenal Self:

THE WARMTH FROM MY LIGHT

This line "It's in the reach of my arms" drew me to our ability to care for others. Serving others by what we actually do is the "reach of our arms". This reminds me of a scripture. The Message Bible puts it best.

> *Matthew 5:14-16, MSG "You're here to be light, bringing out the God-colors in the world. God is not a secret to be kept. We're going public with this, as public as a city on a hill. If I make you light-bearers, you don't think I'm going to hide you under a bucket, do you? I'm putting you on a light stand. Now that I've put you there on a hilltop, on a light stand—shine! Keep open house; be generous with your lives. By opening up to others, you'll prompt people to open up with God, this generous Father in heaven.*

In a world where we are all very sensitive about "our space" this is actually encouraging us to "keep open house" to "be generous with your lives!" That is pretty intimidating and exhausting most days. Even though that is how we may feel sometimes, that's exactly what we signed up for as Christians. In fact, this life is the most fruitful when we are light in dark areas for other people. All too often we are only light around other light. Sundays sometimes resemble a laser show with all the light pinging off of one another at churches all over the world. By Monday, is there enough light where you are, or are you it? Do we always see ourselves as "bringing out the God-colors" where we go? I must admit I don't. Sometimes, I even shrink from "trying to shine" or extending the reach of my arms because I don't want to be bothered. Have you ever felt that way?

What is the reach of your arms? Sometimes a situation calls for you to have a conversation with someone completely unsolicited and unplanned that makes all the difference. Perhaps you were the one in the dark place and needed a friend to encourage you back into a brighter space. The reach of our arms can change the trajectory of any encounter. Let's love on someone for no reason this week. Call someone just because. Actively listen in the conversations you are having and listen for the broken pieces so you can help mend them. By doing so we will as the word says "prompt people to open up with God," starting with us!

Tonight as I write this I'm sitting at the bedside of a dear sister who is fighting for her life. They have started the process of "making her comfortable," but the last words from her mouth to me were "I'm ready, but I don't want to go, I want to live." The only prayer I can think of right now is, "God have your way…your will be done". He knows what is best. She's a beautiful sister with a loving heart and has fought a long painful battle these past few months. As I sit here and think of her infectious smile and her prissy ways I thank God that she felt the reach of my arms when she could feel them and know I was there. As sisters, the reach of our arms is unlike any other embrace. When you know God is tugging at your heart to reach out to someone, do it. You haven't seen them at church, shoot them a text and let them know you missed them. You haven't ran into them at work since you changed jobs; shoot them an email and invite them to lunch. You keep thinking about that girlfriend from high school or college on Facebook that is seemingly going through; don't just comment on the post, pick up the phone. Reach out in some way; whether it's a call, an email, a text or card. Do something to let them feel the reach of your arms tangibly. Tomorrow is not promised. I don't want to have any regrets about a word unsaid. Make the reach of your arms something that can be felt…something that can make a difference…something that can change the trajectory of another sister's downcast spirit. Who do you need to call today? When you really think about it, it's likely several people. Mine is. Just pick one for now. Go ahead…make the call.

Call Log:

Notes to My Phenomenal Self:

PLANK WORK

Thinking of "I'm not cute or built to suit a fashion model's size" I think of how critical we can be sometimes. We can be critical of one another about all sorts of things like body shaming, personality differences, choices of another person – just opinions!!! Every now and then, we need to do some plank work. We need to just take a look in the mirror first and check there. Let's see what the bible has to say about it. *Matthew 7:3 "Why do you look at the speck of sawdust in your brother's eye and pay no attention to the plank in your own eye?"*

Let's do some plank work now. No, not the exercise plank (which I despise) but spring cleaning of some gathered sawdust of specks. I am going to look at my eyes right now. I am checking for specks. Let's see... I am impatient; I tend to over administrate; I have a quick wit and sometimes too quick to respond...just to name a few of my specks.

Plank is defined as *1. A long, flat piece of timber, thicker than a board*. In the scripture it refers to a plank in comparison to sawdust. In other words (my words) sawdust gathered together over time may make a plank. I want us to avoid planks if at all possible. Because if there is a plank in the eye doesn't that mean when a person tried to help with the speck we took it personal and then it turned into a plank over time?

It's no secret that my husband and I are different and thank God. I'm more extroverted and direct. He is more introverted and less likely to point out specks until they have gathered up a bit. As a matter of fact, I believe that is likely one of the issues in a Christian marriage. You both have to live a godly life right there in close proximity to each other with dust specks flying everywhere everyday getting in each other's eyes! (Smile) I bless God for him because no matter what, I believe he points things out in love, not to harm me, but help me/us. I'm not trying to have a plank putting us asunder. (LOL)

AUTHOR'S SIDENOTE: This is my first book. I self-published.
I believe it is likely not proper for me to say (LOL) or (Smile) but this is a great place to say — that's my speck.
I will handle all that in my next book. (LOL) Carry on….

Ladies, just think about it, if we are mutually picking out dust we see "in love" then no one has to walk around with a plank! Let's help each other handle the specks, but giving grace for our own known planks! Speaking of known planks — you know your hot buttons. You know you are super sensitive about your "this or that" so if you have some dust to inspect, be prepared and allow some light dusting coming your way as well. What are your known "planks" that you struggle with? The next time someone brings it up, don't "go off" just say ouch and work it! I am going to leave more room for your reflections on this one. I know I needed a little journal to get it all out! (LOL)

Notes to My Phenomenal Self:

STAY IN YOUR LANE

When I look at the line – "the curl of my lips" I think of keeping my mouth shut. Think of when you have a quick retort to say, but then you just stop yourself and curl that lip. You know this face:

Something stopped you and THANK GOD! That was you staying in your lane. One of the hardest things for women, and let me speak for me, is staying in my lane. You know you think you know better about what someone else is doing or thinking??? There is a great viral video I want you to look for by googling "worry about yourself". The little girl is trying to get her seat belt on and her father says can I help you and she tells him "No you Drive…worry 'bout yourself!" It helps illustrate my point nicely, but I digress.

I have an example. Once I was driving out of town going to visit relatives. During the drive, I was reminded of the fact that I drive so much differently than I used to when I was taking road trips in college. In my earlier years of driving, I would get so nervous when passing an 18-wheeler. I thought it was going to come into my lane and run me off the road. The main reason I believed that was whenever I was about to pass one, I never had my eyes focused on the road in front of me; instead I would have my eyes on the 18-wheeler. Because of that perspective while driving, it always FELT LIKE the truck was IN MY LANE when that was never the case. Now I drive with my eyes on the road in front of me, stay in my lane and pass with caution TRUSTING

THE FACT THAT the other car will do the same, but not focus on that driver at all. Think about it this way - 1 Corinthians 7:17 says, *only let each person lead the life that the Lord has assigned to him, and to which God has called him.*

You see the problem with my driving skills in the example above is that I HAVE LEARNED that when I changed MY THINKING, and what I was focused on when driving, I became a much more relaxed and better driver! Likewise in life the same is true. The bible says in Philippians 4:8:

> *Finally, brothers, whatever is true, whatever is honorable, whatever is just, whatever is pure, whatever is lovely, whatever is commendable, if there is any excellence, if there is anything worthy of praise, think about these things.*

When we keep our mind on what is TRUE (God's word concerning us); what is PURE (thoughts that build and don't tear down); what is HONORABLE (things minding our own business and not that of another); what is worthy of PRAISE (anything opposite of a complaint!) THEN we will change our thinking patterns. We will know when to focus on our lane as opposed to drifting over into another person's lane. It is then we will become better DRIVERS and believe that the other person is NOT COMING OVER TO RUN YOU OFF THE ROAD. You are focused on the life the Lord has assigned to YOU. Focus on that "plan he has for us" and we will be safer, better and more confident drivers.

What is one area where you could do a bit of refocusing? What lane are you slipping over into that has nothing to do with your purpose? What is coming out of the curl of your lips that could reframe the way you see some aspect of your life? Be encouraged and know that what God has for you is for you. Phenomenal Woman…Gurl That's U!

Notes to My Phenomenal Self:

PWT – Phenomenal Woman Testimony

"The stride of my step, the curl of my lips." I've often been told that I'm loud, too loud. I talk loud, I sigh loud, and I even walk loud. I have to say, the description is true. I've been chastised for it more often than not and have attempted to temper my loudness – worked to modulate my tone, become self-conscious about MY BREATH LEAVING MY BODY, tried to step more softly. Until recently, that is. I've decided that my loudness is just one part of phenomenal me and it makes me who I am. I've decided that the stride of my step isn't just loud, it's me walking with purpose. I have some places to be, I have some things to do. I have a directive from the Lord to be bold, to be courageous and not to cower – all because of what He's placed within in me. I can't talk any other way, I can't breathe any other way, and I can't, and WON'T WALK any other way! I've also been told I have a beautiful smile. When someone says that to you, you just smile all the more. Sometimes that smile isn't genuine – it's hiding a broken heart or a broken spirit. And people miss that, because the smile is all encompassing wherever it's bestowed. When it's hiding the brokenness, I've decided that my lips will not curl into a smile – I'll allow the brokenness to show, to share the vulnerability. It's important that others see not only the smile, but also the grimace, the frown, the fear. Only then can they learn to be authentically themselves at all times, wholly living in all the emotions that come with life and recognizing how phenomenal we are in all that we experience. I control my stride and my lips. I'm free to be loud and to be broken and still be PHENOMENAL! **Phenom Dawana Wade**

PWT – Phenomenal Woman Testimony

"Phenomenal Woman, That's Me…"

"Phenomenal Woman, That's Me…" is stated 4 times in the poem. After the reading the poem for the 3rd time in its entirety before writing this piece… that phrase "Phenomenal Woman, That's ME" began to resonate within me. Is the poet describing herself? Is she describing all women? NO, she is describing ME! Phenomenal is an adjective with a definition that states "perceptible by the senses or through immediate experience.

I am a woman who provides an immediate experience that is perceived through your senses. I have the ability to touch your life in a way that provides a lasting impact. WOW. Think about that for a second. In all of my (and your) strength, vulnerabilities, achievements, insecurities, positive impact, setbacks, successes, disappointments, failures, sacrifices, and self-worth …all that I am creates an EXPERIENCE. Even greater than that, I have control over the Experience people have with me. I can be the mean girl, bitter woman, selfish lover, on fire Christian, Ms. Know it all, super mom, overworked/underappreciated mom/wife, stressed and uptight coworker, party girl, social "medialite", trusting friend, SAVAGE, passionate Believer…and STILL choose which what experience I want people to have with me.

I want people to experience AUTHENTICITY! I want you to know that every emotion, conversation, act of kindness, quality time, and word of truth…is coming from a real place. I want you to "feel" me. The last year of my life involved me accepting who I truly am and being my most authentic self. Sounds simple but it's not. I found out really quickly that while people say "Real recognize Real"…in reality, not many can. From "scripted" reality TV shows, deleted social media posts, to copy and paste resumes…we can create an image of what we want people to believe about us that we can't experience for ourselves. You can't give an experience you haven't lived. People can't "feel" the real you when you aren't being you. My challenge to you is that you examine just one area of your life that you can live out your authentic self. Accept yourself first. Experience yourself first. Live your real life first. Being authentically you is only way you'll realize how truly phenomenal you are. And that's the experience you want to give to the world. **Phenom Ericalynn Brown**

Yay! You did it! You made it through the first quarter! What's on your mind? What insights have you made about your SHINE, your lane, your planks, your Real Phenomenal Self?? Do you see yourself in any of our thoughts on the matter? Do you see something different in these lines of this great poem? Just asking…Carry on….

Notes to My Phenomenal Self:

Phenomenal Woman...Gurl That's U!

SECOND QUARTER

I walk into a room
Just as cool as you please,
And to a man, The fellows stand or
Fall down on their knees.
Then they swarm around me,
A hive of honey bees.
I say, It's the fire in my eyes,
And the flash of my teeth,
The swing in my waist,
And the joy in my feet.
I'm a woman Phenomenally.
Phenomenal woman,
That's me.

RAISE YOUR HAND IF YOU'RE SURE!

Confidence! Yes! Confidence! When you walk into a room "as cool as you please" nine times out of ten, you are pretty confident…or are you? Back in the 80's there was an ad campaign for Sure Deodorant and the tag line of the song was "Raise your hand if you're sure!" The song was talking about being sure or confident about the smell of your pits being "good to go" so you could confidently "raise your hands". When you walk into any room as cool as you please, you are sure. You are confident. You are prepared. You know that what's on the other side of that door is handled! On the days when I feel the MOST sure is when I have prayed about it and know I am not walking into any room without my *"surely goodness and mercy following me"*! Romans 8:31 says *if God is FOR me, then WHO can be against me*! That's the best way to walk into the room. There are times I walk in the room and LOOK cool as you please, but on the inside, I am not so sure. Maybe this is you today. Maybe you are shaking in your boots over this or that. Don't sweat it Sis! It's in this weakness God's strength is made perfect in your life. Let him have it. You've got this! When you are feeling less than your best, walking in as cool as you please is a stretch. That's the time to press in and rest in your preparation and the gift on the inside to get this done!

Remember this: Self-esteem is simply the esteem of yourself. It's not dependent on anyone else. Often you hear people say – this person or that person ruined their self-esteem. That's not possible in my way of looking at it. There is always room for us to "encourage ourselves". God commands us to *"love thy neighbor AS YOU LOVE thyself"* in several occasions in the bible. That is the command (loving others). The ASSUMPTION is you love yourself. In other words, that part goes without saying. You show people how to love you by how you love yourself. Take some time to love yourself today. Be sure about the "you" that is walking into every room you enter this week. You can do it! I believe in you!

PWT: Phenomenal Woman Truth

Below are some scriptures that can help with self-esteem

- ✓ *Philippians 4:13: I can do all things in Him who strengthens me.*
- ✓ *Psalm 46:5 God is within her, she will not fall.*
- ✓ *Proverbs 31:25 She is clothed with strength and dignity, and she laughs without fear of the future.*
- ✓ *Psalm 28:76 The Lord is my strength and my shield.*
- ✓ *1 Corinthians 25:10 By the grace of God, I am what I am.*
- ✓ *2 Timothy 1:7 For the Spirit God gave us does not make us timid, but gives us power, love, and self-discipline.*
- ✓ *1 Pet 2:9 But you are a chosen race, a royal priesthood, a holy nation, a people for his own possession, that you may proclaim the excellences of him who called you out of darkness into his marvelous light.*

Notes to My Phenomenal Self:

PWE – Phenomenal Woman Encouragement

"I walk into a room just as cool as you please." Self-confidence is the first thing that ran to my mind after reading this line. It's all about the walk! A person's walk alone can tell you so much about them. It can tell you if they are in a hurry or not, carefree or free spirited, proud or ashamed, afraid or hesitant, worried or concerned, timid or confident. She was aware of others around her but she still chose to be who she was. She wasn't intimidated or arrogant. This is why she said "just as cool as you please" and not as I please. She was saying I'm going to be me and you can perceive me however you like…but I'm going to be me! I find this so encouraging because too many women struggle with self-confidence. This line is saying walk the walk! Hold your head up high and strut your stuff! Be you like only you can! Take ownership of who you are and be proud of it! Own it! Let your walk show just how confident you are in yourself! **Phenom Joy Grundy**

PWE – Phenomenal Woman Encouragement

Hello Beautiful Sister reading this book right now!

This is your moment! This is your Breakthrough!

Do you realize that you have Power within you?

Beautiful Woman, don't be afraid to shine…

Don't dim your light to ease someone else's mind!

You are CONFIDENT! You are STRONG!

You have the courage to be who God created you to be.

You GOT this GIRL! You must know that

You are beautifully and wonderfully created in the eyes of GOD.

So Dear Beloved, walk effervescently knowing that HE who is able to do exceedingly and abundantly more than all you can ask or imagine has given you the power to JUST BE……

So walk into that room as cool as you please,

They don't know how you fall to your knees

THANKING your Heavenly Father for keeping your mind at ease! Beautiful Sister, Stake your claim and stand in position.

Self-Doubt…Not ME!

Insecurity…Not ME!

Low Self-Esteem…Not ME!

Angry Woman…Not ME!

Phenomenal…Phenomenal Woman…That's ME!

Phenom Tia Smith

PWE – Phenomenal Woman Encouragement

The little girl in me, was so desperate for love,
That my heart would go pitter patter, like the heart of a dove.
But young girl let me tell you, those boys are unaware,
Of the diamond placed within you, they really don't care.
Tell them to get off their knees, and if standing to stare,
Very boldly but politely, tell them to
SIT DOWN SOMEWHERE!
Now that I'm older and wiser
The diamond of God shines bright,
I own who God has made me, no guilt shame or fright.
I walk into a room, just as cool as you please,
Because of life's journey, the woman men see,
Is a mystery of sorts, a puzzle to be solved,
Not sure if they should approach or even get involved.
It's the gleam in my eyes, and the furrow in my brow,
They know I'm a child of God,
And to him I have made my vow!

Phenom Pamela Dorsey

----Praise Break---

WOW! Did you feel those three back to back doses of encouragement down on the inside?? It is the perfect time for a praise break! It is a "just because God is good and always knows just when to send me word to boost my day" praise!

Whatever you are dealing with today - THANK GOD FOR WHAT YOU HAVE; THANK HIM FOR WHERE YOU ARE COMPARED TO WHERE you USED TO BE! Just like he took a little boys lunch and fed the multitudes, he can take that little bit you have in this short praise, multiply it to FEED A MULTITUDE!

Thank you God for what it looks like RIGHT NOW!

Right now with my finances!

 Right now with my child!

Right now with my relationships!

Right now with my job!

Right now with my health!

Right now with my emotions!

Right now with every situation that is causing me grief!

Because **I know you are well able** to do exceeding and abundantly MORE than I can ask or think! You will get the glory out of my life and I will be available and able to give your name all the glory honor and praise!!!

Notes to My Phenomenal Self:

PASSIONATE ABOUT MY DREAMS

"The fire in my eyes" reminds me about being passionate about my dreams; passionate about my calling; passionate about embracing my SHINE! Your SHINE can also be interpreted as your gift. James 1:17 in The Message bible says, *so, my very dear friends, don't get thrown off course. Every desirable and beneficial gift comes out of heaven."* We all have gifts. Gifts are God-**given** abilities and strengths that were GIFTED to us to be used to change the lives of others. That's why it's called a gift. When we don't use a gift we dismiss the giver of that gift.

When I was a little girl my great-grandmother (the Original MuDear) raised me in Clarksville, Tennessee. My mom and I spent the summers together until I was old enough to start working (14). My mom lived in the city! I recall loving being in Cincinnati and later in Louisville with her in the summers. I got to have my hair in an afro and I wore the cutest retro outfits! My halter tops were legendary. My mom always had nicest things and gave me gifts of the latest city fashions all the time. I on the other hand was growing up in Clarksville where I was subject to have on buddies or at best the Sears Winner II sneakers at any given time. MuDear was practical if nothing else. She made the distinction between play clothes and school clothes. Anyway, back to my point. Some of my mom's gift choices for me would not always fit my little country girl style. (What did I know at 8???!!?!).

One summer when she came to pick me up, she helped me pack and saw that there were still tags on some things she gave me for Christmas. I tried to hide it but she saw it. She was clearly hurt. Not because I didn't wear it, but because I didn't appreciate it. I felt bad and I pulled that Jordache jean jacket out and put it on even though it was 90 degrees outside!

Likewise when you have God-**given** gifts, and you leave them in the closet with the tags on, it's a direct affront to the giver of the gift. It says you don't appreciate the effort he made to give it to you. God knows the plans he has for us, and he knew exactly what he was doing when he gifted us. So don't leave your gifts in the closet. Instead, use them for the glory of God. Use YOUR gift. Love YOUR gift. Don't try to hide it in the back of the closet like my Jordache jacket. Put some "fire in your eyes" and pursue your dreams!

Notes to My Phenomenal Self:

PWW – Phenomenal Woman Wisdom

"It's the fire in my eyes and the flash of my teeth" What are you most passionate about? There are three things that you need to do in order to make the most of your passion: Be diligent with focused revision, <u>find a mentor</u> that will guide you in the aspects of life that you can't learn traditional ways, and <u>don't allow your emotions</u> to detour your passion. <u>Be diligent</u> in pursuing your passion. You can't be diligent at something without first having a detailed plan. You should reflect on the details of this plan at least twice a year, and revise the plan as necessary. Revision doesn't include changing everything, however, it may result in cutting off friends or making more aggressive advances toward short term goals. Select a mentor that you respect and can be absolutely vulnerable in front of. Listen to their wisdom (both praises and corrective feedback), and study their blueprint. A good mentor is going to challenge you beyond what you consider humanly possible, but don't give up. They have what you need, and truth is they are learning from you. When you are passionate about something, inconsistent idiosyncrasies regarding policy or procedure may find its way into your path. This may cause your blood to boil; however, keep your emotions in check. Remember that drive and purpose for what you do. Recognize and pray about the things you can't change and actively revise that which you can change. Unchecked emotions can be viewed as insubordination and potentially block you from advancing, but stay humble and remember to keep smiling. **Phenom Tirsha Lenior**

DON'T MESS WITH THAT ONE!

When there is a flash of my teeth, there is a smile of assurance. *I am assured that if God be for us, who can be against us? Romans 8:31*

When you have no doubt, you have a smile. Growing up I didn't have siblings. My first cousins were like my brothers and sisters. Life on Cedar Street was an epic childhood. We had each other's back.

My older cousin Tosca was 2 years older than me and when I was in the same school with her I never worried about bullies. I would talk stuff and then schedule her for any fighting that needed to take place. I was not a fighter back then - I used my words. I always felt protected though, because of my large extended family - I always had an uncle or two or seven that would make it known "don't mess with THAT one". It caused me to have a "flash of my teeth".

It is even more comforting and encouraging to read that God is for us! He is in the stands rooting for us when some may come up against us with all kinds of nonsense and foolery! Because he is FOR us, the only time the enemy stands a chance is when God allows it. He knows how much we can bear.

But as we are reminded by Paul, though many may oppose, NONE can prevail against us. God is for us!!! He has taken sides and he is on the side of those who fear him and trust him. God the Father is for his people because he has chosen US, the Son is for US because he has redeemed US with his own blood, the Holy Spirit is for US and he comforts and guides us.

If God himself is for us, who has the nerve, the inclination, or the gall to think they can successfully oppose us? Tell me who??? Dear believer, because the true and living God fights for you this day, none can overcome you! He is up there pointing at us saying "don't mess with that one". Walk in the assurance of that truth today and always because he who keeps us neither slumbers nor sleeps! That's something to smile about.

Notes to My Phenomenal Self:

PWW – Phenomenal Woman Wisdom

"It's the fire in my eyes and the flash of my teeth." This woman was focused and determined and it showed in her eyes. Her purpose ignited her passion and it started a fire. She was burning with this thing. She was going to see the thing through from start to end. I think all these things (purpose, passion, focus, and determination) are qualities that all women should have. We have a way of showing how we feel with our eyes. No one ever showed us how to do it, it was just second nature to us. Some say that you can read a person's state of health by looking into their eyes. It's all in the walk and the eyes! This woman's attitude and perspective was in the right place. This is why she was able to smile, giving a flash of her teeth. A joyful heart is good medicine. Laughter is good for the soul! You can't have these things without smiling! **Phenom Joy Grundy**

PWT: Phenomenal Woman Truth

Scriptures to encourage you to use your gifts!

- ✓ *1 Peter 4:10 As each has received a gift, use it to serve one another, as good stewards of God's varied grace:*
- ✓ *Romans 12:6 Having gifts that differ according to the grace given to us, let us use them: if prophecy, in proportion to our faith;*
- ✓ *1 Timothy 4:14Do not neglect the gift you have, which was given you by prophecy when the council of elders laid their hands on you.*
- ✓ *Romans 12:6-8 ESV / Having gifts that differ according to the grace given to us, let us use them: if prophecy, in proportion to our faith; if service, in our serving; the one who teaches, in his teaching; the one who exhorts, in his exhortation; the one who contributes, in generosity; the one who leads, with zeal; the one who does acts of mercy, with cheerfulness.*

Notes to My Phenomenal Self:

PWT – Phenomenal Woman Testimony

"Phenomenal woman, that's me." The two lines I chose spoke to my very soul. Each time I read them there is a certain attitude coupled with a tad bit of swag when I read them. They make me come alive and believe that I am truly a phenomenal woman. I looked up synonyms for phenomenal and became even more excited. My favorites are extraordinary, extraordinaire, exceptional, uncommon, unique, unusual, exceeding, and atypical. These words explain for me why I have always been different. Why I have always swam against the current. Why I am challenged to follow the ordinary. It is not how I was programmed. It is not the phenomenal me. Those two lines also say loud and clear regardless of my gray hair and my slower gait I am yet a phenomenal woman that's me. It isn't over until God says it over. I must go on and live my dream, my duty, and my life phenomenally. Answering this question for my sister's book made me reflect and remember these vital things about me. I wonder what my life would have been had I known I was phenomenal earlier. I would have understood my thoughts and not wondered why I could not fit in. I would have taken the knowledge of my phenomenal self and pursued my dreams relentlessly, without fear and with an unshakeable faith which would have allowed me to stay the course. To believe you can do what you were created to do is completely mind blowing. So my sisters…. please believe that you can. I can what? Anything God has purposed you to do. Cure cancer? Why not! Rid the world of Alzheimer's? Someone has to do it, so it may as well be you. Save a child through your love and skills, become a wonderful caretaker to many……..the world is your oyster. You can create the most beautiful pearls imaginable. Bring love and peace to a nation, country, a world that is lost……..YES YOU CAN! You can do all things through Christ who gives you strength. Include affirmations in your daily life. I am going to add these two lines that have had a profound effect on me this week. I will start this day November 1, 2017 and I will let you know what the end will be. **Phenom "Princess Neva" Nichols**

Whew! You made it to Halftime! 2nd Quarter of the book is done. What do you think? Not about the book but about your phenomenal self??? What are your dreams? What are you passionate about? What gifts are you cultivating right now? What are you saving your best self for? Note a few ideas now before you move on to the 3rd quarter…you can do it!

Notes to My Phenomenal Self:

Phenomenal Woman...Gurl That's U!

THIRD QUARTER

Men themselves have wondered
What they see in me.
They try so much
But they can't touch My inner mystery.
When I try to show them,
They say they still can't see.
I say, It's in the arch of my back,
The sun of my smile,
The ride of my breasts,
The grace of my style.
I'm a woman Phenomenally.
Phenomenal woman,
That's me.

WONDERFULLY AND FEARFULLY

Before I met my husband, Isadore, I had been living this single life for over 15 years. I had a full single life! I was very involved with the singles ministry at my church. I was completely fulfilled with my life as a mom – always in the stands of the basketball games for my son from 5th grade Jets Basketball to his college ball days. I was completely inundated with my work as Bishop Dudley's executive assistant and other roles and responsibilities at New Life in Christ. My head hit the pillow every night of those 15 years BY MYSELF and fully pleased with myself and whatever I had accomplished that day. It was not easy. There were lonely days. But I knew God was not going to leave me out there. I believe to this day, that is the reason why when my Isadore found me, I was ready for the shower of love that would ensue because I had fully lived and loved me prior to that meeting.

In the poem, it reads "they try so much, but they can't touch". God kept me for sure. Before I met Isadore, my Bishop – Bishop Dudley – prophesied to me at our 10th Anniversary as a church. Four Points Sheraton, in front of 400 LifeChangers and friends, he and First Lady thanked me for the hard work of the event. As a gift they gave me a week in Hawaii in their timeshare! WooHoo! I could hear the waves crashing and I was ready to hit the beach. But then he said, "This trip is for you and your husband for your honeymoon." I was taken aback. First of all there was NO MAN IN SIGHT! I was not dating anyone and no one was on the horizon, because God was keeping me! He had the people in the room point to me and say, "Man coming!" He prayed for me and that was that. I was encouraged. I was exhausted and I was expecting God to work. Three weeks later, I met my now husband, Isadore! We started texting, then talking, then dating, then…well you know the rest. We spent the honeymoon of our dreams in Maui.

Before that line in the poem it says, the men themselves didn't know what they saw. In my case, I was always clear in my OWN MIND who I was. I was always clear that I was saving myself for me. I was always clear about my purpose and the "wonderfully and fearfully" that God created in me. During that 15 year period when men DID SEE me they never said a mumbling word out of line or out of tune, because God was keeping me. Sometimes I wondered what was wrong with me but even in that wondering on my part there was no wandering on their part. I believe as single sisters sometimes we know what's inside. We know it's great! We know it's powerful. What happens sometimes is we tap it down because we want it to be seen on another level (a lesser level) in order to be in a relationship. I want to encourage my sisters who are waiting on God **in any area** of their lives. Don't dim your SHINE – if they can't see it, it was not meant to illuminate that space – move on from there. Don't just take my word for it…keep reading. My God is good…this I know.

PWT: Phenomenal Woman Truth

Scriptures to encourage you while waiting on God

- ✓ *1 Corinthians 15:58 So then, my dear friends, stand firm and steady. Keep busy always in your work for the Lord, since you know that nothing you do in the Lord's service is ever useless.*
- ✓ *Isaiah 40:31 But those who trust in the Lord for help will find their strength renewed. They will rise on wings like eagles; they will run and not get weary; they will walk and not grow weak.*
- ✓ *James 1:12 Happy are those who remain faithful under trials, because when they succeed in passing such a test, they will receive as their reward the life which God has promised to those who love him.*
- ✓ *Micah 7:7 But I will watch for the Lord; I will wait confidently for God, who will save me. My God will hear me.*
- ✓ *Romans 12:12 Let your hope keep you joyful, be patient in your troubles, and pray at all times.*
- ✓ *Psalm 130:5-6 I wait eagerly for the Lord's help, and in his word I trust. I wait for the Lord more eagerly than sentries wait for the dawn; than sentries wait for the dawn.*

Notes to My Phenomenal Self:

PWT – Phenomenal Woman Testimony

"Men themselves have wondered what they see in me." Although I don't try to be, I am very mysterious. I had no idea this is what was being portrayed until I was told on several occasions. People try to figure me out. A lot of times they think they have guessed who I am, only to find out they are wrong. I have learned that I attract people because of a certain grace about me that grasps their attention and keeps them intrigued. It's not a trait that I project purposely, it's really just the type of person that I am. My mysterious ways are formed from past experiences. All of the things I have endured, yet overcame, have shaped and molded me into the woman I am today. I am a survivor! I have survived things that the average person couldn't even begin to fathom. Most would have certainly lost their mind. I've been told that I am admired because of the confidence I have. Oddly, this is told to me by people I barely even know. They say when I walk into a room I command attention. Often being told "there's just something about you". It has taken me awhile to see that there really is something about me. I am my biggest critic. Sometimes it's hard for me to see the things they speak of when I look in the mirror. I feel like I am an ordinary person with a long way to go, then God sends someone to remind me. Now I walk boldly in the confidence that they see in me. I now see it in myself! **Phenom Ebony Wilbert**

PWT – Phenomenal Woman Testimony

"But they can't touch my inner mystery."
I chose these lines because I wish someone really kept it real with me as a teenager and not simply said "don't do it because you will get pregnant" Clearly that wasn't true because I had sex as a teenager and I didn't get pregnant (THANK THE LORD!!) BUT I did have many regrets because of those poor choices. If I could repeat it, I would tell my 15 year old self to hold on to your virginity. It truly is your virtue and you can't get it back. Often our judgement is clouded because we gave our bodies away to boys/men that were never worthy in the first place. Because of poor decisions we hold on to things, people, relationships that were never "supposed to be" in the first place. If he isn't willing to wait for you, he doesn't deserve your inner mystery. I didn't really grasp this until my late 20's early 30's and once I began to walk this out I rediscovered the real me, a phenomenal woman that's me. Then I took an oath of celibacy between me and God and didn't break it until my wedding night. **Phenom LaDonna Hudson**

Notes to My Phenomenal Self:

PWT – Phenomenal Woman Testimony

"They try so much but they can't touch"
As an adult, Maya Angelou's poems have always encouraged me and reminded me of whom I am. When I was single, this passage was occasionally a struggle for me because society painted a picture of how being with someone to feel wanted and whole, was a necessity. Nevertheless, learning the word, remembering who I am, and remembering whose I am reassured me. I knew that the urge to be with someone was just a human feeling and not the blueprint the Lord had for my future. Therefore, saving me for myself became an embedded moral that I lived by. When I met my spiritual parents, Bishop Dudley and First Lady Dudley, I was humbled. Even as an adult I was in awe with the teachings and reminders of the Lord's promises about saving myself for his gift. It allowed me to wait for my mighty man of God, my husband. Today I believe it was the best decision for the woman I became in so many other areas. Saving me for me and being confident in who I am has been a blessing to me in my life and my walk with God.
Phenom Lakeisha Reyes-Wilson

Notes to My Phenomenal Self:

PWT – Phenomenal Woman Testimony

"But they can't touch my inner mystery." People always wonder and try to figure out how I have gracefully lived the life I have. How am I the strong woman that I am? How did I grow up in a house with five brothers? How did I get in such a great school (Bennett College, one of two HBCUs for women) in such a trying time for black women? How do I maintain this beautiful relationship with a husband that is miles away? How am I who I am? People always assume it's something physical that they can touch or a place that I came from that shaped me. My long legs didn't get my degree. My charming smile isn't what makes my long distance relationship work. All those qualities can be touched and since they can be touched – they can be taken away. What cannot be touched, what cannot be taken away is my "inner mystery". My inner mystery is my confidence. My confidence in my faith and the one who created me allows me to feel and live a life full of grace. My confidence, knowing how valuable I am is what makes me strong. My confidence is what I stood on to be bigger and badder than all my brothers and anyone that tested them or me. My confidence pushed me to succeed in school. My confidence shone through on my college application. My confidence is what everyone saw as I walked across that stage, as the first Miss Bennett College and later as a graduate. My confidence in myself, my relationship and the love I give is what has kept my husband loving me every day for the past 27 years. My confidence, they can't touch. My confidence, my inner mystery. My confidence is what makes me a "Phenomenal Woman" **Phenom Rose Hill**

WHETHER OR NOT YOU SEE IT, I WILL BE IT!

In life, we don't always have cheerleaders along the way. In fact, some of the "jeer" leaders spurred you further down the road just proving them wrong. When you have a vision for your life, you are the one ultimately who must see it and embrace it. No matter the obstacles, you have to look for God's favor. You have to look for the "working things together for your good." You have heard that "favor ain't fair". Well I say it is fair for those who are called according to HIS purpose! The line "when I try to show them, they still can't see" is speaking to me: don't try so hard to show them your hand. Just play your hand. Look at Psalms 90:17 *Let the favor of the Lord our God be upon us, and establish the work of our hands upon us; yes, establish the work of our hands!*

Picture this with me as you read: It's Spades night and you have your snacks and the card table and the other team is already talking smack. You see it? This scripture is like playing spades with Jesus as your partner! Let's picture this hand. You have no spades! You have a couple of possible books at best. You know you can't do anything but go board and even then you still might get "set" with this hand that you are playing with. But then Jesus speaks up (interceding on your behalf) and says, "We are going 10for2!" You try to play it off with your opponents but on the inside you are screaming! "What???? Jesus what you mean??? Do you know what I have in my hand!?!?" Jesus is like "just play your hand. We got this." So you are making moves. You are trusting him and when the opponents start to play that Ace of hearts that just beat that queen you had…your one possible dream in your hand…BAM Jesus is cutting that mess up with a spade! Do you see it??? Now that's your book. Your dream again! Finally, you are down to your last cards and you don't know how you are going to make it. Do you see it? You trust Jesus and he shows you he also has BOTH JOKERS in his hand. They can't do anything to you without him allowing it! Whew! You thought you were set! You thought you would renege but you just played your hand and THE MASTER OF THE SEAS heard your despairing cry! The Lord established the work of your hands by playing his in concert with yours. With Jesus as your partner you are beating the odds all the while.

I said all of this to say – it doesn't matter what "they" see or what "you" see – you still CAN BE whatever was in your hand to be all along! But don't just take my word for it, keep reading….

Notes to My Phenomenal Self:

PWT – Phenomenal Woman Testimony

"They try so much but they can't touch my inner mystery. I was raised in New York. Around the age of 8, my mother got caught up in the crack cocaine epidemic that swept our communities and for the first time since slavery, took black mothers away from their children. We ended up homeless and I chose to go live with my Dad. Within a couple of years, he also got caught up in the epidemic, and as a result some horrible things happened in our family. During those years from age 8 until about age 14, there was so much out of my control and happening to me and my family that made me feel dead inside. I felt like everything had been touched, and ruined. Filled with shame, I set out on a mission to prove my worth and my family's worth to make up for all the bad that happened. It took a while, but with God, I'm learning that what was in me could not be taken away. I'm learning that it didn't need to prove itself, that it just was. The only person who needed to know and see that was me. The lines of this poem express a deep wisdom unfolding in my life. When I self-talk to that young woman I was then, it goes something like this – You were so confused and believe that what happened to you, made you. The struggle of your family and parents made you look for everything and anything outside of yourself but what God put in you could not be touched it could not be destroyed by storms and struggle, in fact storms and struggle made you stronger. So, likewise my sisters, life will try you, but it can't touch you; it can't touch what God put in you. Remember this when you feel you have nothing or mistakenly believe you are nothing. You may try to show them so you can believe it yourself. If they can't see…that's okay, just make sure you can.

Phenom Dietra Wise-Baker

PWT – Phenomenal Woman Testimony

"They try so much but they can't touch my inner mystery." For eight months I was in an abusive relationship. The person I thought I knew turned into a complete stranger. Right before my eyes he no longer looked the same; his skin got darker, his hair grew nappy, and his eyes had no light in them. It was as if the toxic spirit inside him started to take physical form – brokenness, self-hate, insecurity, jealousy. His "I love you" turned into "I hate you". There were new accusations every day. I never knew what side of him I was going to get. No matter how hard I'd try to stay one step ahead of him and his mind games, I always fell short. It was always my fault. I never did anything right. I became his enemy. He tried so hard to break me. How dare I have fun, enjoy life, and be happy when he was unhappy with himself and his circumstances. What he didn't know was the inner joy I had was God, and that my God is bigger than any situation. Sometimes we do the right things for the wrong people and no matter how hard we try to win them over to see how genuine we are, we lose. But that loss is often times a blessing. Forgiveness is truly for yourself, the other person doesn't matter. It is a disservice to yourself to give someone in your past the power over you in your present and future. Don't give up on love because of someone who's last name you won't even remember five years later. Don't give up on life because of one bad moment. Just because they can't see what is inside you doesn't mean what is inside you isn't great.

Phenom Gabrielle Locke

PWT – Phenomenal Woman Testimony

"When I try to show them they say they still can't see. " This passage reminds me of the years that I spent wondering if I had any inner mystery at all. I spent too many years wondering what anyone could see in me. It was crushing to my spirit. I often felt so small. What could any man see in me? I wasn't tall or cute and I'd been told I sounded like a man with my deep voice. Strangely at the same time I knew there was something deeper inside me, something wonderful and valuable. But how was I ever going to believe in my own mystery when others couldn't see it? Maybe I was wrong and there wasn't anything worthy or special or mysterious inside of me? This passage also reminds me of the long struggles in my career for recognition. I knew I had talent. I knew I was gifted and deserved a seat at the table but my voice at times was ignored. How often I tried to show my inner mystery, my natural excellence but they still couldn't see. Finally I got it! Just because they don't understand and can't touch or see my inner mystery has nothing to do with the reality and power of my brilliance! Just because you can't see it doesn't mean a thing! It's all there baby! It's always been there. I say, It's in the arch of my back, The sun of my smile, The ride of my breasts, The grace of my style. I'm a woman phenomenally… **Phenom Carol Daniel**

PWE – Phenomenal Woman Encouragement

Phenomenal Woman…That's Me

As a current Lieutenant Colonel in the U.S. Army, one would never have known that a girl who was raised in the baddest projects of Portsmouth, VA would ever obtain this rank or status. Oh yes, the roads were very hard, rough even. The enemy had placed obstacles from being molested by four different family members prior to the age of thirteen to discrimination in and out of uniform in my way to keep me from my destiny! But God had greater in store for me - A Phenomenal Woman is what I was destined to be! So to every little young girl or lady, I'll declare, that no thing, but you can keep you from your destiny. Be like me and peek into your destiny. There you will find all that God has designed you to be. To my sisters reading this, I will say, "Girl, hold on…the best is yet to come! Stay your race! Don't get off course! Your blessings are racing your way! God made you different…a beautiful woman, phenomenally!" Now as a Lieutenant Colonel leading this man's Army, God has set me in a place of honor. I shall remain humble, for he gave me charge over young men and women to guide and direct and to be a godly example! **Phenom Valeria Johnson**

Notes to My Phenomenal Self:

DON'T GET WEARY – JUST GET AT IT

My daughter Carmen is such an inspiration to me. She is a single mom with three children. She told her daddy (my husband Isadore) she wanted to be a comedian and she started to pursue her dreams in St Louis. She did fine, but she knew LA was the place to be if she wanted to success. She didn't get weary, she just got at it. He encouraged her to go for it and took care of her children while she just got at it. It has not been an easy road, by far! However, today, she not only supports herself and her children as a full-time comedian, she is now a Boutique owner too. This was another dream she had that she just made up her

mind about one day and three months later she was having the grand opening to Sugar B's (located at 1421 Chambers Road in St Louis by the way). She just did it. Easy? By no means! Setbacks? Surely, but nothing insurmountable. When you purse the phenomenal, you must learn how to maneuver the setbacks and see beyond them to your dream fulfilled!

> Galatians 6:9-10 says *Let us not lose heart in doing good, for in due time we will reap if we do not grow weary. 10So then, while we have opportunity, let us do good to all people, and especially to those who are of the household of the faith.*

It's so easy to get weary. One moment, you get encouraged, "yes I can do this" and run home with bursts of energy to do this that and the other and boom. Some distraction causes weariness to set in.

You wake up in the morning....it's a good day.... you head out to work to get 'er done and you get there and only two of the 20 things on your list get done because distractions cause weariness to set in. You make a plan "I'm going to the gym starting Monday" and all day Saturday you prep your meals for the week...you get your cute workout gear laid out and then Tuesday morning hits and weariness sets in. Have you ever done the budget to get debt free and out of nowhere clearance sale emails and texts from your creditors (who only giving you this price when you use that 27% credit card) are distracting you and weariness sets in.

The issue as I see it is that we keep putting hope in OUR ability to act. Move your hope to your availability – not ability. If you are available, the hope in the Lord and HIS ABILITY is what keeps any of us rising up daily and get it cracking! I know it's tough. If that's you today don't get weary. See all those things you planned were going to bring God glory so the enemy did his job by sending the distraction but ultimately you have the power. Use it to maneuver those distractions. Feel his Holy Spirit and allow it to strengthen you to mount up and feel renewed.

Let's take a lesson from all of the testimonies, observations and other encouragement of this 3rd quarter! I hope God is showing you some new things about yourself...things he put in the original design. You don't have to run from it or alter it. The original manufacturer would have a problem with you messing with the "wonderfully and fearfully". No need for adjustments or recalls or consulting third-party designers. No need to re-gift the gift or abdicate the call. Go to the source. Learn from the source. You can do it Phenomenal Woman...Gurl That's U!

----Praise Break----

Psalms 145:1-3 says *I will exalt you, my God the King; I will praise your name for ever and ever. Every day I will praise you and extol your name for ever and ever. Great is the LORD and most worthy of praise; his greatness no one can fathom.*

Repeat this Praise:

In every situation I am facing YOU ARE still God. You can make a way out of no way. You can turn the situation around to actually find something for my good. All things are working together. My future is blessed. The fruit of my womb is blessed. Your word will come to pass concerning them. I will move out of your way God and let you be God. I will praise you in it…through it…and on the other side of it!!

Repeat this Prayer:

LORD, help me lift my voice to you today--and every day--to acknowledge you and thank You for all you have done for me. You are good and your mercy endures forever! As I meditate on who you are, what you have done, what you have made, and the awesome, unfathomable power you possess, I realize I cannot even comprehend all that you are. You are truly wonderful and I thank you for loving me and caring for me. In Jesus' name, Amen.

Notes to My Phenomenal Self:

FOURTH QUARTER

Now you understand
Just why my head's not bowed.
I don't shout or jump about
Or have to talk real loud.
When you see me passing,
It ought to make you proud.
I say, It's in the click of my heels,
The bend of my hair,
The palm of my hand,
The need for my care.
'Cause I'm a woman Phenomenally.
Phenomenal woman,
That's me.

BE IT UNTO ME…AS YOU HAVE SAID

In this last stanza of the poem, Maya says you "understand just why my head is not bowed." For me this is highlighting the fact that there is no need to hang my head when I am just carrying out what the Lord said about me. We talked about that wonderfully and fearfully made – that was said about you before you were even born! Walk it out…head not bowed. Look at *Luke 1:37 - For no word from God will ever fail."*

In this scripture the angel of the Lord was telling Mary that she was going to conceive Jesus. His last statement to her was… for nothing is impossible with God. He told her a number of what seemed to be impossibilities and then he told her the clincher sentence. He told her who God was! It is outside of the nature of God to fail. What I love is Mary's response. The very next verse says…*Luke 1:38 - "I am the Lord's servant," Mary answered. "May your word to me be fulfilled."*

She didn't need to go consult her girls… she did not need to go see if Joseph was okay… she just received the word of the Lord. Her head was not bowed even though she was about to be the talk of the town! In her response, she identified herself. She said, "I am the Lord's servant." The King James Version says, "*let it be unto me as you have said*". In other words, everything that you said about me that the Lord said about me…let THAT be unto me.

So fast-forward 2000 years later to your situation and my situation. Whatever the Lord is saying about you…that's what's up! It's not about those lies that the haters are saying about you. Everything that the Lord our God has purposed, let it be unto you. Everything that he has promised…let it be unto you. Everything that he has destined for

your life, hold your head up and let it be unto you. It's about you knowing who you are, articulating it in a proper response, and then walking in the grace that he has afforded us.

REPEAT AFTER ME: I am the Lord's servant…may it be unto me as the Lord has said!!!! Then they will understand just exactly why your head is not bowed!

Notes to My Phenomenal Self:

PWW – Phenomenal Woman Wisdom

"Now you understand just why my heads not bowed." I've lived. I've had triumphs and failures. I've had successes and lessons learned. Through them all, I've learned that I am human; I will make mistakes; I will fall down; but I will always get up and become better than I was yesterday. I will adjust my crown, learn from my mistakes, and keep pressing forward. At no point will I stay in my failures (or allow anyone else to keep me in them); and boy have I had some; in business, love, friendships, you name it!! BUT, once I remembered who I was and whose I was, I lifted my head. **Phenom Shaneal Clayborne**

PWE – Phenomenal Woman Encouragement

"I don't shout or jump about or have to talk real loud." The more confident I become in myself the more I understand the importance of being able to command attention without having to say a word. As I come into who I am as a woman, I enjoy being able to say something of importance without actually having to say a word. As I tell me clients: "If you ever find yourself in a place where you are fighting to be seen or heard then you are in the wrong place. It is then your mission to find "your place". I can tell them this with certainty because, although I have never been one to beg for attention or to be seen, there was a point where I would fight tirelessly to be heard. **Phenom Shaneal Clayborne**

HOW YA LIVIN' – BY FAITH

Back in the day, the late Bernie Mac used to say "Who you wit?" In the poem, "Now you understand just why my heads not bowed" is a great question. The answer…because of who I am with! I am living by faith that all the things God has for me and mine are coming to pass. My head is not bowed because I am winning! By faith!

Look at Psalms 18:30. *It says, As for God, his way is perfect: the word of the LORD is tried.* What an understatement to us today! In this country, we are being tried like never before. There is "Breaking News" at the bottom of the MSNBC every night when I come home. But we have history with God. Our heads are not bowed because we are not living by what we see on the news but by Faith! In this passage - David had less evidence than we do!

God's Word has been tried, tested, scrutinized, and relied upon by Christians throughout the ages. And, just as David testified, they have found it more than sufficient for their every need. They have discovered, in every generation and in every hard circumstance, that God's Word truly is perfect.

His counsel is always wise, his history is always accurate, his lessons are always true, and his commands are always relevant. God's way is perfect. David was not merely making an observation or teaching an academic lesson; David's point is that because God's Word has been tried and tested by millions through the centuries, and has been found perfect, each of us should therefore build our lives on this tried and sure foundation. Fred Hammond sings a song called Perfect and True! Pure in all your ways… (YouTube it)

Who do you look to for direction and for advice? When we want to bow your head remember we are a people of great faith! Don't trust popular opinion, what's trending on Twitter, or well-meaning friends, just look to the hills where your help comes from. If you are looking to hills, guess what?? Your head is not bowed! Just go to God's perfect Word over and over again, for counsel in every area of life to keep your head up. Every area. Even those areas you think you have under control. Yes that one.

The Word of the Lord is tried, it is proven, it is sure -- but have you tried it? What word are you believing God for today? Don't. Bow. Your. Head. Trust God…and trust what he put in you.

PWT: Phenomenal Woman Truth

✓ *Matt 21:22 Whatever you ask in prayer, you will receive, if you have faith.*

✓ *Romans 10:17 So faith comes from hearing, and hearing through the word of Christ.*

✓ *Hebrews 11:6 And without faith it is impossible to please him, for whoever would draw near to God must believe that he exists and that he rewards those who seek him.*

✓ *Hebrews 11:1 Now faith is the assurance of things hoped for, the conviction of things not seen.*

Notes to My Phenomenal Self:

PWT – Phenomenal Woman Testimony

"Now you understand just why my heads not bowed." Throughout my life I struggled with my identity, pleasing others and the shortcomings that made me feel less than my true worth. Unfortunately, these things allowed me to adapt a terrible trait of being a control freak and becoming my own "worse critic". It reminds me of the negative cycle I have overcome and the continuous faith in God to be proud of myself when life is not going exactly how I want it to go. I do not have to be a reflection of what I may be going through. The simplicity in just "holding my head high" and not allowing it to bow is a great way not to give attention to negativity or bad circumstances. We have a tendency to run to the nearest girlfriend or person that we know will entertain the negativity in our lives. I believe we have to learn how to be quiet and not feed the downfalls that may occasionally surround us. Whether it's other people, the enemy, or myself - whatever is coming against me as an opposing force - I do not have to react to it. I can simply hold my head high. That action allows me to exhibit a unique poise, class and most importantly the best characteristic and trait of a phenomenal woman!! **Phenom Tyisha Wise**

PWT – Phenomenal Woman Testimony

"I don't shout or jump about, or have to talk real loud.

When you see me passing, it ought to make you proud."
Ugly, fat, black, bald, ghetto, angry, controlling, man less, lazy, bad attitude bitch, uneducated, broke, classless, clueless… and the list goes on. These are just a few of the things African American women are called in this society. Yes, I'm speaking as an African American woman, because it's not just who I am, it's what I am. What we…the "we's" that look, think, and act like me…are perceived to be is determined by who is not only doing the looking, but those who are also part of the being. I am a black, beautiful, educated, elegant, interesting and intelligent woman. Unfortunately I get held down and back by the views of those who …well…who don't look like me. But don't get it twisted, this story…my story is color blind and can refer to any women depending on the box someone is trying to put them in or keep them out of. As women, we too dehumanize, degrade and categorize each other down to the lowest point of humanity. We forget we share a common bond, a common thread and a common notion. We are women…hear us roar! Instead, we jab and punch, bob and weave, kick and run into the hands of yet another person; another so called sister friend, boyfriend or even a mirror. These only reiterate the aforementioned negative stereotypes, emotions and feelings of this society; false though they may be. But I am a Phenomenal Woman! I am not some uneducated ghetto hood rat on welfare. Nor am I some classless hutchie revealing more than I'm concealing. *"I don't shout or jump about, or have to talk real loud. When you see me passing, it ought to make you proud."* Why? Because I am a

Phenomenal Woman. This line reminds me that while there may be a few lost and confused women out there, the vast majority are striving with our heads held high to be the best woman, mother, daughter, sister, niece, wife and friend we can be. We work hard, play harder, and love the hardest. Society should be so proud and recognize us more than try to keep us, still in this day and age, as second class citizens. More importantly, we should be proud of each other, respecting our differences and emphasizing our similarities. We are Phenomenal Women! **Phenom LaChelle DuBose**

PWW – Phenomenal Woman Wisdom

"I don't shout or jump about or have to talk real loud." When I read those two lines, they encourage me to be confident in who I am as a person. I am not a loud, boisterous person but work hard at what I do. I used to admire the people with a big personality and assumed they are the only ones that would get credit for their hard work. But then I remembered, I'm not working to please man. Everything I do is to please and glorify our Heavenly Father, not man. God will fight my battles for me. If I am to be recognized for something I have done, it will happen. When I received that special recognition or award, God received all the credit because I can do nothing without Him. **Phenom Sonya Rayford Cage**

DON'T JUMP AND SHOUT…JUST SHOW FRUIT

In the poem it says, "I don't jump and shout and talk real loud". Truth is, I am loud. I don't want to be known for being "loud and wrong" but fruitful and productive. In John 15:2 it says, *"He cuts off every branch in me that bears no fruit, while every branch that does bear fruit he prunes so that it will be even more fruitful."* I made up my mind about this one thing, because it is time to have some fruit on the vine of our lives. We have prayed about it. We have been prophesied to about it. We have had several confirmations. Now it's time to act. Now it's time to DO!

Have you ever notice how the 80-20 rule stays alive and well? 20% of the people doing 80% of the work and vice versa? That's because those who are always churning out fruit at home, at work, at church, at school are being pruned to bear even more fruit. Beware of being busy rather than being fruitful. Sometimes we are BUSY in areas but yet not fruitful. You just need to be available to be fruitful. If you avail yourself, you can be fruitful in your relationships, in your job, in the marketplace, or in ministry….wherever THAT area is. Just START. Look up this song and listen for some motivation.

- "Wish That" by B. Reith

Let us stop waiting for the conditions to be just right. Let's stop giving excuses why we woulda shoulda coulda and just DO IT. When we move, God will move. Oh and if you're already just doing a lot of things right now, this is not encouraging you to do more necessarily. It is encouraging you to cut those things off that are not producing fruit and do the things that will. Time is of the essence.

PWE: Phenomenal Woman Encouragement

"When you see me passing, it ought to make you proud" When I was younger I was shy and wasn't confident. I was complemented but, never really paid attention to the complements. It was actually hard to accept complements. I looked at me and my life and didn't really think that everyone else had struggles as well. I didn't really share my life for fear that someone would use it to hurt me. After I went through things in life, people told me later how it gave them strength to watch what I went through. It gave them strength seeing how I carry myself after finding out what I've been through. You are fearfully and wonderfully made. Stand tall. Be proud of who you are and the beautiful design of God. God has blessed you with beauty inside and out. We are forever a work in progress but, never let someone put their idea of beauty on you. You were made to love and be loved. Everyone has a story and a past. No one's life is perfect. Focus on the good of the lessons and the power of your strength. No matter what life throws at you, you will adapt and overcome. The struggles of life come to make you appreciate and enjoy the peace and blessings. People need you to live on and tell your story. They need for you to be encouraged so, that you may encourage others. You have so much to give and it will be given back to you. Open up to the world around you and allow yourself to be limitless. Girl you are phenomenal! **Phenom Lisa Perry**

PWT: Phenomenal Woman Truth

Scriptures to encourage you to bear fruit.

✓ *John 15:1-27 "I am the true vine, and my Father is the vinedresser. Every branch in me that does not bear fruit he takes away, and every branch that does bear fruit he prunes, that it may bear more fruit. Already you are clean because of the word that I have spoken to you. Abide in me, and I in you. As the branch cannot bear fruit by itself, unless it abides in the vine, neither can you, unless you abide in me. I am the vine; you are the branches. Whoever abides in me and I in him, he it is that bears much fruit, for apart from me you can do nothing. …*

✓ *Genesis 1:28 And God blessed them. And God said to them, "Be fruitful and multiply and fill the earth and subdue it and have dominion over the fish of the sea and over the birds of the heavens and over every living thing that moves on the earth."*

✓ *Galatians 5:22-23 But the fruit of the Spirit is love, joy, peace, patience, kindness, goodness, faithfulness, gentleness, self-control; against such things there is no law.*

Notes to My Phenomenal Self:

PWT – Phenomenal Woman Testimony

"When you see me passing it ought to make you proud." Living in a life of betrayal, abuse and mistrust, self-confidence was a far reach for my inner being. My head hang low, and my voice was muffled with pity. I shuddered at the idea of attention—I just wanted to be. Overhauling the injustices from early in life, my solace remained in the Love of one being...one true friend...one who loved unconditionally...my Heavenly Father. Trusting in man was not an option for me. Trusting in the One who can erase pain and hurt was the last recourse for me if I was to survive what I perceived as a cruel world. Years of intense self-reflection, sacrifice and relentless searching for a deeper relationship with our Father, paved the way for me to overcome adversity, poverty and a broken spirit. Achieving my goals with perseverance, endurance and tenacity was my loud talk. What I despised, made me stronger. Who I hated, I learned to love. What I desired, God granted in abundance. My life in poverty did not halt my acceleration to make something of myself. I never leaned on man, but leaned on the only Father I ever knew—our Heavenly Father. God granted me the favor to rise above shame to become a confident and fierce woman. I strive to model good behavior in front of my young sisters. Modesty and humbleness reflect my boldness in God's love. I hope my achievements make my young sisters very proud. **Phenom Dr. Marcella B. Sancho, DNP, RN**

PWT – Phenomenal Woman Testimony

"When you see me passing, it ought to make you proud." As the first person in my family to join the Air Force, I left New York and for the first time, I was 3,000 miles away from home. My second assignment was also 3,000 miles away from home.

The military wasn't on my list of options, but it was one of the best decisions I've ever made. My first assignment was Zaragoza AB in Spain. I was assigned as an Operations Officer in a flying squadron I was involved in several base functions which were not directly related to my job. Once on an evaluation I was marked down by my supervisor, however the Base Commander was an endorser on it and marked my evaluation up. You see, I didn't "have to talk real loud" but my work spoke for me over the years. Living in Spain I visited about 10 countries, to include Germany, France, Switzerland, London, Greece, Morocco and Holland just to name a few! From commanding over 700 airmen in Los Angeles AFB to Knoxville and finally arriving at Scott AFB where I would retire. After almost a year I was asked to find another job, because I was told I was a square peg in a round hole. After working in another position I was awarded HQ Company Grade Officer and was pictured in the base newspaper right next to the person who told me to find another job, **that's how God works!** I'm not extraordinary but I've been blessed to see and do some extraordinary things. I'm so grateful for that! When you go through a few things it will either make you stronger or break you. As a Black woman, I'm proud of what we've accomplished in spite of all the other things that go on to try to crush our spirit. You don't have to be loud. Just accept yourself and be proud of who you are. Currently and for the past 20 years, I am an AFJROTC instructor at a Soldan H.S. in St Louis. I've had the opportunity to share my experiences in the military in hopes of helping some of our youth realize they can achieve what they want if they start to realize how gifted and powerful they really are. **Phenom Deborah Sims**

PWE – Phenomenal Woman Encouragement

"When you see me passing it ought to make you proud" There's an inner strength within a woman that exudes in the different things she does. We are the only creatures on earth that come so close to death during child birth. We are some powerful beings. We are all created in God's own image. The same God that created the heavens and the earth, the stars and the skies created us. If we could somehow keep this thought in the back of our minds we would understand that there isn't anything we can't do. The words "When you see me passing" aren't just for when other people see me, but when I see myself….when I look in the mirror and see the reflection looking back at me. I should see strength, power, beauty, love, peace, joy, and over-comer. I should be proud at the reflection looking back at me. No I'm not perfect and I'm not trying to be. I just want to be the best me that I can be. If God made two of us the same, one of us would be useless! Ladies, embrace your individuality, embrace your flaws, embrace your imperfections, and embrace ALL of you because God makes NO mistakes. As you see other women passing it should bring a smile to your face or within. To see another woman doing her thing, making moves, living life, should make you feel empowered. It should make you feel proud to be a woman. We have to continue to lift each other up and not tear each other down. We are all talented in our own right. Let's celebrate our curves, culture, hair textures and lengths, ups, downs, strengths and weaknesses, quirks, and all of the above. Let's celebrate womanhood! **Phenom Sharona Ward**

NOW WHAT?

We are in the 4ᵗʰ quarter! We are at the end of this book, but that is not the end of the story, much work has to be done. The book is coming to a conclusion but it not the end of the message. It took me a year to finally get this book done. There were stops and starts along the way. Facebook memories (some days it is the accuser of the brethren) would not let me forget what I committed to – writing this book. My 4ᵗʰ quarter questions for you are as follows:

1. What are you prompted in your spirit to do?
2. What do you have on the back burner?
3. What vision have your wrote, made it plain, but it is still not yet speaking?
4. What area is not producing fruit right now, but you KNOW it should have some buds on the vine?

Don't let this year go by without making it happen! It took me a year, and I didn't quite do it the way I wanted but I did it. You have had to excuse several "published work no-no's" but – it's my first book (LOL).

Hebrews 11:6 says, "*And without faith it is impossible to please God, because anyone who comes to him must believe that he exists and that he rewards those who earnestly seek him.*" I heard a song once that said this: "If you pray, don't worry and if you worry, don't pray." The song simply stated what this scripture states to me. If you are going to believe God then believe God. If you are going to pray then don't negate your prayers by then speaking negatively about what you have placed before the Father. If you are going to believe God for big things; if you going to trust Him to do the things that he is able to do, then you must have the faith to believe in the God you're praying to. If it is impossible to please God without faith, then we should watch what we say after we pray. If you are believing God for your healing but you also always worrying and saying woe is me in the next breath. What is your God-sized prayer today? What else are you saying about it? If you have put some negative thoughts out with the prayerful thoughts, trade those for faith. All you need is the measure you have. You can stand on that. Your measure of faith and his promise is all you need for God-sized prayers to be answered!

What's next? I am adding an appendix to get started on the "what's next". You didn't just pick up this book by happenstance. You didn't just buy this book to support me (although I so appreciate it). You were ready for the Phenomenal to be called out in you. You ARE ready because it's time to walk it out. Commit to 3 things.

- Write out a plan for what's next for you!
- Get a mentor who is gifted in the area of your plan.
- Choose someone to mentor in an area where you are gifted.

Paul said "*Follow my example as I follow the example of Christ.*" (I Cor. 11:1) "*Whatever you have learned or received or heard from me, or seen in me — put it into practice.*" (Phil. 4:9) In other words, he is saying "let me mentor you. Let me be your role model. That's why we need both a mentor and a mentee. Who are you allowing to model for you? A person that can speak into your life is a vital relationship to have. Don't make any excuses, just do it. Look up this song and listen for some motivation.

- "The Master's Calling" by Deborah Joy Winans

The first song is looking back and wishing you had done things differently. The next one is encouraging you to listen for God's voice calling you. Your "what's next" plan will help you bring clarity to what you heard him say.

In 1 Samuel 3:7-10 it says:

> …..*Now Samuel did not yet know the LORD: The word of the LORD had not yet been revealed to him. The LORD called Samuel a third time, and Samuel got up and went to Eli and said, "Here I am; you called me." Then Eli realized that the LORD was calling the boy. So Eli told Samuel, "Go and lie down, and if he calls you, say, 'Speak, LORD, for your servant is listening.'" So Samuel went and lay down in his place. The LORD came and stood there, calling as at the other times, "Samuel! Samuel!" Then Samuel said, "Speak, for your servant is listening."*

Many of us when using a cell phone have learned the skill of "selective answering." Our cell phones ring; we look at who is calling, and in an instant decide whether or not we are going to answer. You can now send an auto text back or just DECLINE. It is "selective answering."

Unfortunately, too often we do something similar when it comes to when God is calling us. We use "selective listening." When we read what God has to say in the Bible we think, "Go ahead and speak, Lord. I will think about what you have to say to me. We read the word, we hear the word, and because it's just like God he will even send a confirmation! That's his way of saying CAN you HEAR ME NOW?
If it is a hard word, we may act like we didn't hear the phone. Maybe it was on silent. If it's a word of correction we act like it's just voicemail we left unanswered. When it's a promise or a blessing, though, we are at full attention and even have a special ringtone for it so we don't miss that call. Samuel did not yet know the Lord. So listening is not a skill for a seasoned saint. We just have to quit our stalling tactics…clean out the voicemail and start returning calls! Get to know all his ringtones so when that call comes…you will be there to take the call!

PWT-PHENOMENAL WOMAN TESTIMONY

I have one last story. As I have stated throughout the book, I ALWAYS KNEW who and what I was supposed to be. I grew up in the church and always wanted to serve the people of God. In the 3rd Grade, when asked what I wanted to be when I grew up, I answered – THE CHURCH SECRETARY because "she wore nice clothes and got to tell people what to do". I loved everything about working in the church office and seeing the results of our work during the week manifest itself on a Sunday morning. Even back then, I knew one was leading to the other. One day something was said to me that was extremely out of line in this place that I held so dear (the church). I left and didn't look back. I went from being there multiple times a week to not being there at all for any reason. The next time I came to church from that day was for MuDear's funeral in my sophomore year in college. No one touched me or physically hurt me in any way but their words were powerful enough and wrong enough to turn me away from the things of God for many years. I went to church off and on after graduating from college, but never had the connection to it that was needed to cultivate the calling on my life.

My life took a number of twists and turns that lead me to my calling. Following along this journey a lot happened, but all of these events brought me full circle.

After my son Charles and I moved from Dayton, OH, I never dreamed it would mean I would eventually divorce. But my job transferred me to Scott AFB where I was invited to the chapel by the woman who would later be the Mother of my now church, the late Mother Ree Myers. She adopted me into the chapel family and I rededicated my life to Christ there. While at the chapel, I jumped right into serving.

Phenomenal Woman…Gurl That's U!

Singing in the choir; teaching in youth ministry (YES); children's choir director and of course, ministry administration needs. Each of these roles are closely aligned with my calling. While at the Chapel, I went on a road trip to a conference in New Orleans called Woman Thou Art Loosed where I received the gift of the Holy Spirit and spoke in tongues for the first time. But something was missing. Although I was serving and connected to lots of people I cared about, I was tired of getting close to military people who would go on to the next duty station and have to have those hard goodbyes. I was tired of relying on a set of orders to determine who my "chaplain" would be. So in 1999 I decided I was going to start looking for a church off base. But then Chaplain Dudley came to Scott Gospel Service. He called a meeting with all the leaders and asked us to serve with him to make Chapel 2 the best it could be. Then he said something I never would forget. He said, "Oh by the way, the word chaplain is not in the bible, I'm your pastor." I had not called ANYONE pastor since I left the church that Friday between high school and college. I called him Pastor from then until I called him Bishop Dudley. My calling as an administrative professional in the kingdom started that day. New Life in Christ Interdenominational Church formed in 2003 and we have been changing lives ever since! You see when I left the church back in 1986, that was meant to harden my heart toward the things of God and for a period of years, and it did. But God has a way of bringing you to your expected path. That moment was meant to make me distrust the position of pastor so I could never be in the position I am in today – the honored role of serving my Bishop and

83 | Page

First Lady. Bishop Dudley has always shown me the greatest respect and I call him my spiritual father. Coming to O'Fallon, IL was never on my dream sheet of locations, but it's where I flourished like never before in the call on my life.

Likewise, you are on a path. There may have been setbacks like myself and many of other ladies have described in this book. We were about to give insight from our stories. Lots of us have had some twists and turns. The poem was a great motivator to show you how phenomenal you are and what you can do, but it's just a backdrop. The real power is in the wonderfully and fearfully that God placed in you from the start. The wonderfully and fearfully I kept referring to is from *Psalm 139:14 I praise you because I am fearfully and wonderfully made; your works are wonderful, I know that full well.* Motivation came from my contributing writers and myself through our stories and wisdom and testimonies and encouragements. But the power is in the truth of the word of God that was found throughout. I didn't know how to write this book without it. It is the foundation of who I am. You see, my sister, we are PHENOMENAL WOMEN but Jesus is the real Phenom! We are all just taking lessons from him day after day!

It is my sincere prayer you were inspired by my words and the words of the other sisters that inspired you throughout. Mainly I pray that the word of God spoke the loudest and made the greatest impact for you!

There is one part of the poem that is repeated 4 times. It bears repeating now. YOU ARE a woman…Phenomenally…Phenomenal Woman…Gurl That's U! And when I see you passing it makes me proud!

PWT: Phenomenal Woman Truth

Psalm 139:14-16 The Message (MSG) 13-16 Oh yes, you shaped me first inside, then out; you formed me in my mother's womb. I thank you, High God—you're breathtaking! Body and soul, I am marvelously made! I worship in adoration—what a creation! You know me inside and out, you know every bone in my body; You know exactly how I was made, bit by bit, how I was sculpted from nothing into something. Like an open book, you watched me grow from conception to birth; all the stages of my life were spread out before you, The days of my life all prepared before I'd even lived one day.

Notes to My Phenomenal Self:

Appendix A: My Plan for Next Steps

Tips for making your plan for the next steps:

1. Choose one area, even if there are many. Don't try to solve everything right now. First of all, everything is not even off track. Choose one thing for now.
2. Do something. Before the week is out, do ONE ACTION toward your plan.
3. Set specific milestone dates. Don't just say, I am going to do IT this year. You may not start until the end of the year if you do that. (I am a witness)
4. Pray. Take your plan to the Lord and ask him to help you stay on track and open doors for the resources you may need.
5. Tell someone. Pick a friend who will hold you accountable. Tell them what your milestone dates are so you can have a clear timeline to check in. Don't post it on Facebook if you are not serious (LOL)
6. Reward yourself. When you hit each milestone have a planned celebration for yourself also planned.
7. Keep working on the plan. No matter how many stops and starts you have, go back to the plan and continue to work the plan.
8. Don't give up. Never give up. Even if you have to change/tweak the plan, stay on course.

<u>Next Steps Planning Page:</u>

Appendix B: Tips for Choosing a Mentor:

1. Be clear about why you want a mentor. Are you looking for someone to offer specific advice? Do you want a conduit to your industry's movers and shakers? Or do you just need a sounding board?

2. Define your personality and communication style. What kind of mentor would best complement you? You may choose someone who's your opposite (an extrovert to your introvert, for example), or someone in whom you see yourself (and vice versa).

3. When asking someone to be your mentor, explain why you're asking and what you'd expect out of the relationship (see No. 1). Name your reasons for approaching this particular person. Don't be afraid to be flattering (e.g. "I'm asking you because you are the most successful person I know").

4. A mentor is a powerful role model. Look for someone who has the kind of life and work you'd like to have. Also, choose a mentor you truly respect. Don't just go for the biggest name you can find.

5. Before asking someone to be your mentor, consider first simply asking for input on a single specific topic. How did that go? Was it good advice? Was it delivered in a way that made sense to you, and filled you with confidence and energy?

6. Look for ways you can reciprocate the help your mentor offers. At the very least, you can occasionally spring for lunch or, say, send a fruit basket. You don't want to be all take-take-take.

7. Show gratitude. Never let your mentor feel taken for granted! Also, supply feedback. If your mentor suggested something that really worked out for you, report back. People love hearing about their part in a success story.

8. When looking for a mentor, think beyond former bosses and professors. Look to older family members or friends, neighbors, spiritual leaders, community leaders, the networks of your friends and colleagues, or officials of professional or trade associations you belong to. Avoid asking your direct supervisor at work. You want to be free to discuss workplace issues as well as your plans for future advancement.

9. Keep in mind that mentoring can take many forms. It can be a monthly lunch, a quarterly phone call, a weekly handball game, or merely a steady E-mail correspondence. Your mentor does not even have to live in your city or region.

10. Many mentors derive pleasure from "molding" someone in their own images—great for them and great for you if you want to be molded. But beware of mentors who are too bossy, controlling, or judgmental. This is your path, not theirs.

11. Don't become too dependent on your mentor. The idea is that one day you will eventually be able to fly on your own. In fact, you may not take every bit of advice your mentor offers. Continue to think for yourself.

12. Guess what: You're allowed to have more than one mentor. In fact, you can have a whole committee if you want, and call it your Board of Directors. Choose different mentors for different facets of your professional (and even personal) life.

13. Finally, if you ask someone to be your mentor and that person refuses, don't be hurt or offended. This is not personal! Potential good mentors are very busy people. Thank him or her for the consideration, and ask for a referral.

Source: https://money.usnews.com/money/blogs/outside-voices-careers/2010/01/13/13-tips-on-finding-a-mentor

Appendix C: Tips for Choosing a Mentee:

1. Don't overthink it. There is likely some young woman that you are already in relationship with at work or at church that fits the bill – you just haven't considered what you are doing as mentoring.

2. Pray for the right fit. Ask God to show you who needs what you have to give. When he does, be open to the possibilities.

3. Allow it to be organic. Don't walk up to the young woman and say, "I choose to mentor you." Just ask her to accompany you just doing life (getting nails done, grocery shopping)

4. Choose one for now. Don't come out of the gate trying to do too much, and then end up doing very little or nothing.

5. Let the mentoring begin! Once you have had an initial meeting, meet again. Decide together what this time together should be and allow it to evolve naturally.

6. Don't overcommit. Don't promise what you cannot provide.

7. Don't rescue. As the senior person in this mentor/mentee relationship, you are not Jesus. You are not the momma. You are not the police. You are not here to save the day.

8. Advice based on your experience IF ASKED, but don't tell them what to do. Your life is the example. Allow it to play out in front of them.

9. Listen. Be present. Let the mentee guide the conversation. Read between the lines – listen for what is not said.

10. Find the phenomenal in them and celebrate it. Be aware of their likes and passions and don't assume you will share the same. Champion their SHINE!

AFTERWORD

Thanks for reading my first book! My next book is not far behind and it is called "Phenomenal Woman…Gurl That's U: Letters to My 15-Year Old Self". It is written to encourage and empower young ladies between the ages of 13-20. It will be a daily devotional/journal. The same contributing writers from this book wrote letters for this project as well. Thank you again Rev. Dr. Dietra, Ericalynn, Sonya, Shaneal, Carol, Elder Pamela, LaChelle, Natasha, Joy, Lashonna, Rose Marie, Valeria, Tirsha, Lisa, LaDonna, Gabrielle, Neva, Dr. Marcella, Dianne, Deborah, Tia, Dawana, Sharona, Ebony, Lakeisha, and Tyisha.

Thanks again to my husband for getting me a desk for our room so I could write late at night or early in the morning without going very far! Thanks to my family for allowing me to tell ONLY A SNIPPET of all of our stories. There are lots more to come! Stay tuned! Check out my blog at www.dagnelistening.blogspot.com when you get the chance or my website www.dagnebarton.com for upcoming news.

Dagne

CONTRIBUTING WRITERS BIOS

Thanks to my GURLS who said yes to my request to contribute their thoughts and encouragements derived from the poem by Maya Angelou. I am so glad your voice is speaking through this book along with mine! I appreciate your time and never ending encouragement of me always! Kudos and thanks to each of you! Phenomenal Women indeed! (Listed alphabetically below)

- **Rev. Dr. Dietra Wise Baker** is a phenomenal woman currently serving as Chaplain and Program Director with incarcerated youth in the Saint Louis, MO region. She also serves as a community organizer working on breaking the school to prison pipeline. Dietra is married to Cornell and they have one beautiful daughter Alexis Baker.
- **Ericalynn Brown** is a Phenomenal Woman who is a mother to 3 little people, a servant leader in the community, and woman in pursuit of God's heart. She is a phenomenal woman who considers every hard place, challenge, opposition, set back, and pain as a good thing because it gives her live purpose and gives glory to God (Romans 8:28)
- **Sonya Rayford Cage** is a phenomenal woman who is an Air Force military spouse, mother, and Air Force veteran. She is from Mascoutah, IL and graduated from Mascoutah High School and went on to receive a Sociology degree from the University of Illinois, Chemistry degree from SIUE, MBA degree from Webster University and currently a Ph.D. Candidate in Business from Capella University. Sonya spends her time supporting the military spouses and families. She is also a member of the sorority Alpha Kappa Alpha, Inc.

- **Shaneal Clayborne** is a phenomenal woman who was born and raised in East Saint Louis, IL. Her passion is assisting other women cultivate their gifts and walk them out. When she is not helping her clients Glitz, Glam, & Go For It, she is mentoring young adults, volunteering in the community, and serving at church. If she could only imprint one message on the hearts of others, it would be that through your imperfectness, you are still worthy… and you will ALWAYS be enough. #Glitz #Glam #Go

- **Carol A. Daniel** is a phenomenal woman who is first and foremost a mother and wife. She and her husband Patrick are celebrating 23 years of marriage. They are the proud and exhausted parents of two sons, one an engineer and the other an actor and photographer. Carol is a 35 year veteran of broadcasting, an award-winning radio news anchor, reporter, newspaper columnist and television talk show host. Carol is a gifted motivational speaker and author of the book, "All I Ever Wanted. Relationships, Marriage, Family". She is the 2017 President of the Greater St. Louis Association of Black Journalist, board member of the YWCA and a member of New Life in Christ Interdenominational Church in O'Fallon, Illinois where she along with her husband, spearheaded the couple's ministry, "Journey to Oneness" for nearly a decade.

- **Pamela Dorsey** is a phenomenal woman whose journey in life has become the pages by which she has authored poems and written spoken word encouraging many. She is the "Nana" to three gorgeous grandsons and mother to a courageous son and two inspiring daughters. God has blessed her in ministry, education and her career having served over 26 years in the military. Now, this is her season to give back what God has so graciously given her. Be Inspired!

- **LaChelle DuBose** is a phenomenal woman who serves as the Executive Assistant to Bishop T. Anthony Bronner of ELIM Christian Fellowship of Buffalo, NY, as well as Music Director over the Worship and Fine Art's Department. She is also the Executive Director of Turning the World Upside Down Covenant Fellowship, an ecclesiastical organization which encompasses over 15 churches/ministries throughout the United States. LaChelle is a graduate of the State University of New York at Buffalo with a B.S. Degree in Interdisciplinary Social Science's-Health and Human Services as well as in African American Studies. LaChelle has a heart for God and his people, and considers her relationship with him as uncompromising.

- **Natasha Edwards** is a Phenomenal Woman that knows the Power of God! She an Army Brat that benefited from the diversity. She loves arts and craft; in her spare time makes jewelry. She is a graduate from HBCU, Central State University who has excelled in the Federal Government. When she was younger, she thought I would be a nurse.

- **Joy Grundy** is a phenomenal woman who…loves and serves God wholeheartedly. She gives credit to Him for all of her accomplishments. She is the proud mother of two boys. She has a passion for working with young children and is currently pursuing her Bachelor's degree in Early Childhood Education. She enjoys writing and plans on publishing some of her work one day.

- **Lashonna Harden** is a phenomenal woman whose passion in life is to help eliminate any barriers that prevent students from attaining life success in the areas of academic achievement and in emotional development. She graduated with a B.A. in Business from Eastern Illinois University and after a life changing experience volunteering for Lutheran Social Services in Champaign, IL, she went back to Eastern and received her M.S. in counseling. Lashonna is happily married to Dr. James Harden, PhD. and are proud parents of two beautiful children, Shaun and Nina Harden. In her spare time, she enjoys spending time with family, reading, swimming, looking for DIY projects, as well as volunteering in her community. *(submission in "Letters to My 15-Year Old Self" – coming in late March)*

➤ **Rose Marie Hill** is a phenomenal woman who, a South Carolina native, is a Senior Human Resources Specialist with the FDIC. She has worked/lived in Italy, Germany and Doha (Southwest Asia) and travel to other countries to include Spain, the Republic of Czechoslovakia, France and Africa. Rose has a great passion for being a servant. She works diligently in her church and has always made time to give an encouraging word to young women. Happily married for 27 years, Rose attributes much of her success to the support she receives from her husband, Quinn Hill. She also believes that three of her biggest fans are her two daughters, DelShaun and Quinn and granddaughter, Jasmine.

➤ **Valeria Johnson** is a phenomenal woman who loves God with all of her heart! Raised in the thickets of P-town, VA, Val was determined to overcome poverty and the obstacles of life to make a better life for herself, family, and others! Today she is a Lieutenant Colonel, aiming to be a General Officer, in the Army! She enjoys spending time with her lovely family, working in the church, community and mentoring others, especially young people, to be the best they can be! Most of all she likes to have fun, living life to the fullest!

➢ **Tirsha S. Lenoir** is a phenomenal woman who is the proud mother of 2. She was a teen parent and knows the value of mentoring young women and men about the many choices as teens that will shape your life. She is a native of New Orleans and is a teacher. She also volunteers with her church as a teen ministry leader.

➢ **Lisa Perry** is a phenomenal woman who didn't allow mistreatment as a kid to allow her to walk in unforgiveness. She didn't allow the world around her to tell her who she could and couldn't be. She decided that she would give up her life of freedom to take care of her sister's kids when she walked away without a good bye. She is the responsible one that her family knows they can depend on. Daily she decides to put God and his plan for her life above all things.

➢ **LaDonna Hudson** is a phenomenal woman who was born and raised in East St Louis, IL. She currently resides in Swansea, IL with husband Joey and two sons Major & Jaylon. She has a BA in Human Resource Management from Lindenwood University and a MA in Rehabilitation Counseling from Maryville University. LaDonna is currently employed by Wells Fargo as an Employee Relations Consultant. In her spare time she enjoys traveling, working out, volunteering at her church & spending quality time with family & friends.

➢ **Gabrielle Locke** is a phenomenal woman who is twenty-two years old and is currently enrolled at Northern Illinois University studying Athletic Training. She was born in Belleville, IL to a teacher Cherise Locke and a retired technical sergeant of the military Wheeler "Bernard" Locke. For about seventeen years, she was dedicated to dance and learning different styles such as ballet, modern, and tap. Now, her passion has transitioned into her education about her major. Wherever life takes her she strives to make her mother and now her guardian angel, her father, proud.

➤ **Neva Nichols** who is a phenomenal woman (recently discovered) will now begin embrace life as a phenomenal woman. I will be excellent in what I do because I have been practicing for many years. Now is the time to execute and implement. Mediocrity is no longer an OPTION!

➤ **Dr. Marcella Sancho** is a phenomenal woman who grew up in North Philadelphia, PA. Shortly after graduating from high school, Dr. Sancho enlisted in the U. S. Coast Guard before accepting a commission in the USAF Nurse Corp. Dr. Sancho spent most of her professional career completing education endeavors with an Associates from BAC, BS then MS in Nursing from St. Louis University, MO. She completed a Master's in Public Administration from Keller Graduate School of Management and Doctorate in Nursing Practice from Chamberlain College of Nursing. Dr. Sancho is currently a Visiting Professor at Chamberlain College of Nursing and Care Coordinator and Patient Educator at Memorial Hospital East, Shiloh, IL. She attends New Life in Christ Interdenominational Church, O'Fallon, IL since 2003 and serves in the Worships Art Ministries.

➤ **Dianne Shelton** is a phenomenal woman who has a strong sense of who she is; she believes in the strength and the courage of the human heart. She's very loyal in friendship. Dianne has the utmost concern for young girls as they grow in this day and ages environment. I'm praying that all phenomenal women would take up the charge and encourage the life of one young lady.

- **Deborah Sims** is a phenomenal woman who is a retired Air Force officer and currently working as a junior reserve Officer training Corps instructor at a high school in St. Louis where she has impacted the lives of 100s of cadets. She's also an entrepreneur, event planner and real estate broker. She's from Brooklyn New York and has traveled extensively and she looks forward to traveling more after she retires from the SLPS system.

- **Tia Smith** is a phenomenal woman who loves inspiring young girls to be the best they can be. She is purposely transparent of her struggles she has experienced with body images in hopes that it will encourage other women to JUST BE. She has a passion for learning and pushing beyond her comfort zones. Tia has found true love with her husband Kenneth Smith and their four children Kayla, Kellan, Kendal and Kole who resides in Belleville, IL.

- **Dawana L. Wade** is a phenomenal woman who resides in Nashville and is the mom of two adult children, Nathan and Dorian. She has many years of youth and leadership development experience and currently leads Salama Urban Ministries, serving youth and families in the greater Nashville community. Dawana is a member of Kairos Community A.M.E. Church and Delta Sigma Theta Sorority, Inc. She has served on a number of boards and is a mentor to a number of youth and adults.

- **Sharona Ward** says, "I am a phenomenal woman because I'm flawed and I'm ok with that. My strengths and imperfections make me who I am. I love hard, care deeply, and laugh often. I am a single parent, a friend, a sister, a daughter, a God chaser, and lover of all things natural just to name a few. I want to touch as many young girl's lives in my lifetime so that they can know how phenomenal they are!"

- **Ebony Wilbert** is a phenomenal woman who is a Lover of God and heavy praying believer. She is the mother of two wonderful boys. She is a friend, a daughter, and a confidant to many. She is Texas made and Missouri raised. But most important to her, she is family oriented.

- **Lakeisha T. Wilson** is a phenomenal woman who works for University Medical Imaging, as a Radiology Technologist and Assistant Supervisor of Medical Imaging. This led Lakeisha to aspire to be a leader in the community with a focus on setting a positive example for teen girls. Passionate about education, she completed an AS in Logistics and BS in Healthcare Administration in 2014. She in heavily involved in the community as a member of Alpha Kappa Alpha Sorority, Inc., Black Girls Run, Greater Sacramento Urban League Young Professionals, and much more. She is a devoted wife to her husband (Cedric B. Wilson) of 12 years and mother of one son, Keith Cole Jr. Lakeisha believes that all things are possible through prayer, perseverance, and preparation, an everlasting life-lesson, which she learned from her beloved mother and spiritual parents (Bishop Geoffrey V. Dudley, Sr. and Lady Glenda D. Dudley).

- **Tyisha Wise** is a phenomenal women who is no stranger to encouraging and uplifting women and youth of today's society.. Due to the hardships she faced as a teenager and young adult, her compassion for youth and God's people grew tremendously. After serving with many ministries and youth programs throughout the years, Tyisha is excited and forever grateful to God for allowing her to participate in the Kingdom Agenda on earth. She is a devoted wife and mother of three lovely children and resides in the great Metro- East area in Illinois. Because of her passion for healing and helping people she is pursuing her degree in Psychology and hopes to add this credential to her list in the near future.

AUTHOR BIOGRAPHY

MRS. DAGNE BARTON is a wife and mother, sister to many, & LifeChanger to all she meets. She is a passionate woman about God's business in her many roles. She has a Bachelors in Business Administration from Austin Peay State University and a Masters in Non Profit Leadership from Webster University. Dagne is a consummate professional as Executive Assistant to the Bishop and Pastoral Ministries and Projects Director at New Life in Christ Interdenominational Church.

She lives in O'Fallon, Illinois and is happily married to her God-sent husband Isadore Barton. She has successfully raised one son, Charles Coleman Joy, and is excited to be mom by marriage to Ron, Carmen, Cameron, Cayelon & Cayla Barton. She has devoted her life to her family and to the calling on her life for the ministry of administration at New Life and beyond. She is a proud soror of Delta Sigma Theta, Inc., a Mary Kay Independent Beauty Consultant and has formed a staff and ministry development/training organization called ValUAdded Consulting. Finally she is a mentor to multiple young women – two through Project Graduation; and others personally chosen at New Life and in the community. She is making an impact, and setting the example in her home as a wife and mother; in her church as a leader and encourager; and in her community as a LifeChanger, author and mentor. *"God will let you laugh again; you'll raise the roof with shouts of joy!"* - *Job 8:21 The Message Version*. Phenomenal Woman…Gurl That's U! is her first book.

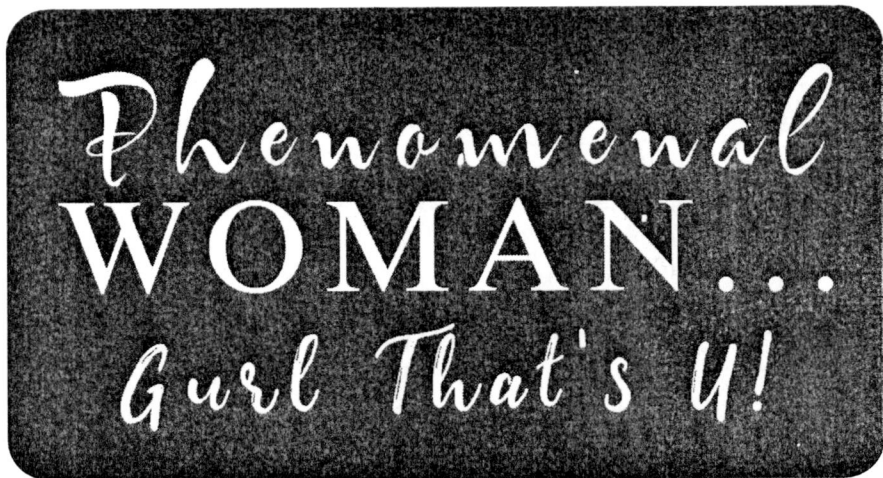